DEALING WITH
DEPRESSION
IN 12 STEP RECOVERY

DEALING WITH
DEPRESSION
IN 12 STEP RECOVERY

by Jack O.

GLEN ABBEY BOOKS

Published by Glen Abbey Books, Inc.
All rights reserved.

Cover design by Graphiti Associates, Inc., Seattle,
Washington

Library of Congress Cataloging-in-Publication Data

O., Jack.
    Dealing with depression in 12 step recovery / by
    Jack O. — 1st ed.
       p.   cm.
    ISBN 0-09-412513-9
    1. Depression, Mental. 2. Twelve-step programs.
    I. Title.
RC537.015   1990
616.85′.2706—dc20   90-14047

Printed in the United States of America
10 9 8 7 6 5 4 3 2 1

DEDICATED TO

SHARON WOODS, M.D.

Contents

Introduction

Very few, if any, can say they have not been depressed or gone through periods of sadness and unhappiness. Our individual 12 Step recovery programs will not protect us from negative events happening in our lives. Our program can and will help us in dealing with depression.

This book illustrates how many of us have been helped with our depressions. We have learned to accept and work through our negative feelings, deal with the "here and now," and change our attitudes and behavior. We have come to see that our program, our Higher Power, and our willingness teach us ways to deal with our thoughts, our feelings, and our actions.

—Jack O.

1

Depression: Definition and Types

First of all, we need to come to a definition of depression. The word "depression" has become such a part of everyday conversation that it means something different to everyone. People use "depression" to express everything from feelings of sadness to thoughts of suicide. The word "depression" also has different meanings to counselors, psychiatrists, and psychologists.

Put as simply as possible, the definition, various types, and symptoms which are important for 12 Step members are as follows:

Definition

According to *Webster's Ninth New Collegiate Dictionary*, depression is: "A state of feeling sad, inactivity, difficulty in thinking and concentration, a significant increase or decrease in appetite and time spent sleeping, feelings of dejection and hopelessness, and sometimes suicidal tendencies."

SYMPTOMS

The symptoms of depression, as presented by the National Institute of Mental Health, are:

- Persistent sad, anxious, or "empty" mood
- Feelings of hopelessness, pessimism.
- Feelings of guilt, worthlessness, helplessness
- Loss of interest or pleasure in ordinary activities, including sex
- Sleep disturbances (insomnia, early morning waking, or oversleeping)
- Eating disturbances (loss of appetite, weight loss or gain)
- Decreased energy, fatigue, being "slowed down"
- Thoughts of death or suicide, suicide attempts
- Restlessness, irritability
- Difficulty concentrating, remembering, making decisions

At times, depressive disorders masquerade as persistent physical symptoms that do not respond to treatment, such as headaches, digestive disorders, and chronic pain.

When someone in recovery says, "I'm depressed," do they usually fit into the above definitions? Let us first look at the different types of "depressions" most often associated with recovery.

"EVERYONE HAS IT" DEPRESSION

All too often a person will say they are depressed when in fact they are only reacting to events all of us go through. This is usually called "reactive depression" or normal mood changes brought about by loss, stress, burnout, or unhappiness with current circumstances; i.e., relationships, job, financial problems, etc. We are all human beings facing daily, complex life issues and events, and will experience sadness.

When an individual gives up alcohol, drugs, or any addictive substance, behavior, or dependency, there will naturally be a period of depression. When something which has been a big part of our lives is given up, we naturally go through a period of grieving over the loss. Although our addiction has had negative consequences, we still react with sadness. Only when we accept our addiction can this specific type of sadness and grief be over.

"STINKING THINKING" DEPRESSION

This type of depression is usually described as negative imaging, depressive personality type, emotional depression, or psychological depression. By using the term "stinking thinking," we describe the depression and also make it easier to understand for those in recovery. The phrase "stinking thinking" is common in all 12 Step Fellowships. It illustrates quite clearly that our thoughts need to be corrected.

This type of depression is characterized by distorted, irrational, negative and incorrect thoughts about ourselves, other people, places, and things. The way we live, act, and perceive our lives is related to our thoughts. When we are depressed, we add to our depression and stay depressed because we only "see" the past, present, and future as negative, dark, and gloomy. Not working to correct our character defects adds to our negative thoughts.

Many members report that this type of depression or negativity began long before their addiction or dependency. They felt they never really "fit in" and may have used alcohol, drugs, or food to feel "normal." They now accept the fact that much of their negative self-talk and most of their character defects were survival skills learned as children.

BIOLOGICAL DEPRESSION

When we speak of biological or clinical depression, we are referring to an imbalance of chemicals in the brain which regulate feelings, thoughts, and behavior. Current research also points to genetic links, with biological depression often occurring in families.

"STUCK IN RECOVERY" DEPRESSION

This type of depression visits almost all 12 Step members during recovery. It can happen not only when we begin our program but also after many years of sobriety, abstinence, and spiritual progress.

The most common symptoms are confusion over our progress, lack of faith in and energy to work the 12 Steps, boredom, frustration, anger, and a general "don't give a damn" attitude toward the Program and fellow members.

The above four types of depression will be discussed as we get into the other sections of this book. To conclude, depression is a normal reaction to things we all experience and is not necessarily all that bad. It's part of our makeup as human beings.

On the other hand, it can be crippling, whether it is from a lifetime of negative thinking or from an imbalance in brain chemistry.

We are all going to experience depression. Some of us will have different types of depression during our lives. Others will have different types at the same time. Let's look now at the various ways we contribute to depression or sabotage ourselves: signs and signals of depression to watch out for.

2

How We Contribute to Depression

Danger Signs, Signals, Self-Sabotage

The following are not in any special order of importance. They are comments from members I interviewed about what set off, added to, or prolonged their depressions in recovery.

Isolating

The easiest way to stay depressed is to isolate: stay by yourself and don't seek help for your depression. A member said to me, "When I feel lonely, I prefer to be by myself." Isn't that true? It is far more positive to say, "When I feel lonely, I need to seek out and be with other people."

INACTIVITY

When we "just sit there," unwilling to do anything which may help us out of depression, we are only thinking about ourselves. We focus on our shortcomings, past mistakes, lack of friends, the ways people, places, and things have mistreated us, and the general "awfulness" of our lives.

STOP GOING TO MEETINGS

Attending our 12 Step meetings is one of the most important aspects of recovery. We are repeatedly told how important meetings are, but it is only too easy to "drop out" of this activity when we're depressed. Just as risky is attending only speaker meetings, sitting in the back row, and not participating. When we cut out meetings or just attend and don't say anything, we are cutting ourselves off from those who may help and understand our depression.

NO SPONSORSHIP

We don't want a sponsor, and we don't want to be a sponsor.

TRYING TO FIGURE IT ALL OUT

Staying inside your own head, thinking, thinking, thinking, is a sure way to add to and prolong depression.

"Why am I depressed?"

"Why am I not 'normal'?"

"Why don't I have a life?"

"What's *wrong* with me?"

Even if all the answers were known, even if all the specific reasons we are prone to *be* depressed and *stay* depressed were known, we would still have to make some effort to work through and out of depression.

WAITING FOR THE MAGIC WAND

How many of us have said, "Things would be better *if only* . . ."

When we're depressed, many of us "wish for" people, places, and things to be different. We forget our Program is for day-to-day living. Improvement comes by our efforts on a day-to-day basis. We could have a long wait if we are sitting around wishing for some magic in the future to make us happy.

DIET AND EXERCISE

"What difference does it make what I eat when I'm this down?"

Eating the wrong foods and making no effort to get any exercise can greatly contribute to depression. Also, skipping meals, not keeping ourselves and our living quarters clean, and neglecting ourselves physically prolongs our down times.

SELF-PITY

When we are on the "pity pot," demanding constant attention and sympathy from others, we can't make much progress. Self-pity is a "smokescreen" we hide behind when we are unwilling to help ourselves. It can be a cover-up to disguise anger, resentment, fear, envy, guilt, impatience, and procrastination. Most importantly, it is often a sign of self-centeredness.

We are sometimes too proud to admit we are depressed and need help. When pain overrides self-pity and pride, then we can seek help from outside ourselves.

IMMATURITY

Chronological age makes little difference when we discuss immaturity and depression. Many of us have carried childish egos and immature attitudes into our adult lives. We have difficulty giving up child-like needs for control and a desire that all our needs be met. An attitude of *I want what I want when I want it*, and wishing for power, attention, and instant pleasure can add to and prolong our depressions.

EXPECTATIONS

Recovery teaches us to face reality. We need to make fewer demands on ourselves, others, and life in general. When we expect others to know our needs with no effort on our part, or expect to be given all the good things in life simply because we think we deserve to have them handed to us, a lot of sadness and destructive confusion follows.

COMPARING, NOT IDENTIFYING

When we *identify* with another person in our recovery program, we bond with that person. In so doing, we share the message and benefits of recovery.

When we *compare* our progress with others, we break that bond and become separated by an act of our own ego. We easily get down on ourselves when we keep score and expect a report card or a diploma for working the Steps.

NEGATIVE SELF-TALK

The way we talk to ourselves is the easiest way to evaluate whether we are adding to our own depression. Someone once said, "I have met the enemy and it is me," and "Would I let anyone else put me down the way I put myself down?"

Self-hate makes our character defects worse. If we talk to ourselves as losers, we stay losers. Many of us have done this so long we don't realize we're doing it.

PLAYING GOD

The game we always lose is trying to control people, places, and things. We can find no peace when we are trying to force everyone and everything to be the way we want them.

When our overinflated ego is directing our thinking and behavior, we set ourselves up to be disappointed. When we play God and are into our control and manipulative games, we become overdependent on outside forces to make us happy.

RECOVERY MASK

When someone is wearing a "recovery mask," they deceive others into believing they are doing well in the program. The real danger lies in deceiving themselves into believing they "have it all together." They're depressed and stuck in their recovery program, but won't let anyone know what's going on.

When we only share our opinions, attitudes, and advice instead of what we're feeling deep down inside, we are likely to keep our depression active.

The above self-sabotaging signs were the most frequently mentioned when interviewing 12 Step members who have worked through their depressions.

3

PERSONAL STORIES
(THE WAY OUT IS
THROUGH)

LIFE IS FAIR
(NINA K.—2-1/2 YEARS)

Recently my sponsor of two years told me I have been making marked improvement in realizing what I know and what I don't know. When I first came into the program there were a lot of things I thought I knew. My delusions of reality, and especially of myself, told me I was almost an expert on just about any given subject. My expertise included education, employment situations, love, relationships, sex, marriage, children, etc., etc.

Ironically, these were the very things about which I felt so sorry for myself—the things I was depressed about. I had once had all these people, places, and things, but for some strange reason (certainly not me!) I no longer had any of them. In my first months of recovery I believed I was a victim of this cruel and unfair world.

Gradually, I have gotten a second chance to learn about reality and myself. I have been given back many of the people, places, and things I traded away for my addiction. It was strange to me at first, but now it is easier to understand: I didn't get any of them back until I was ready to admit I knew absolutely nothing about dealing with them.

My tendency is still to want to run or blame, but thanks to my growth in the program, I have learned in most cases that "I am the problem." When pain and anxiety come my way, instead of becoming and staying depressed I am choosing to ask for help.

KEEP COMING BACK
(FRANK J.—11 YEARS)

When I had my tenth anniversary, I thought I'd finally arrived. My "thinking I'd finally arrived" gives a good idea where my head was on that occasion.

What took place then was a period of terrible depression and getting really stuck. I became dissatisfied and began to find fault with meetings and the people at them. I rationalized that I'd been in the program so long I had better things to do with my time than go to meetings. After all, it had been a long time since I thought about drinking. I deserved a break.

I'm still a little shocked that I could slip away from the program and back into classical depression so easily. I forgot I had a *progressive* disease, and one that tells me I'm not sick. No matter how many 24 hours I've been sober, I need to keep hearing the message that my answers and peace of mind come through working the 12 Steps. Keep coming back!

RET Helped Me
(Jean N.–8 years)

I was introduced to the principles of Rational-Emotive Therapy (RET) when I was in treatment for alcohol and drug addiction. I spent most of my first year in recovery working the Steps the best I could. I got a lot of help from my fellow members and my sponsor.

I reread the literature on RET, and started to work on the negative belief system which produced so much of my stinking thinking. It's just my opinion, but I believe much of the depression we go through and hear about from friends in the program has to do with the way we deal with our upset feelings.

Howard Young, in his pamphlet *A Rational Counseling Primer*, states that:

> Self-defeating ideas remain so when they are accepted without question. If you vigorously and consistently question and challenge the ideas and beliefs behind your uncomfortable feelings you will discover that, in time, you will become more and more free of negative emotions.

In other words, if you truly put in effort and lots of practice, after a period of time, the probability is that:

1. You will not get **as** upset.
2. You will not get upset **as often**.
3. You will not get upset **as long**.

SUMMARY:

Insight #1

Upsetting feelings come from upsetting ideas.

Insight #2

You stay upset because you keep telling yourself upsetting ideas over and over again.

Insight #3

Conscious effort and hard work will overcome upsetting ideas. You do this by constantly challenging and uprooting irrational ideas and replacing them with constructive, sensible ideas.

Using RET wasn't 100% of the answer in helping work through my depression, but I have gained needed insight into how I talk to myself. I don't "should" myself as much any more. I'm more comfortable when I make a mistake, and don't quickly jump to everything "being awful."

ANTIDEPRESSANTS
(DALE M.—6 YEARS)

My first year in recovery was spent mostly just hanging on, not working on much except staying away from alcohol and drugs. I had received what now seems good advice: A complete look at my depressions wasn't possible until I was clean and dry for one year.

After that year, I went to a psychiatrist for an evaluation. My family had a long history of depression, and I was still being plagued by mine. I was instructed to begin treatment with an antidepressant. I was anxious about taking any kind of pill now that I was in recovery.

My sponsor gave me a pamphlet entitled *The A.A. Member—Medications and Other Drugs*, which states:

> Because of the difficulties that
> many alcoholics have with drugs,

some members have taken the position that no one in A.A. should take any medication. While this position has undoubtedly prevented relapses for some, it has meant disaster for others.

A.A. members and many of their physicians have described situations in which depressed patients have been told by A.A. [*sic*] to throw away the pills, only to have depression return with all its difficulties, sometimes resulting in suicide. We have heard, too, from schizophrenics, manic depressives, epileptics, and others requiring medication that well-meaning A.A. friends often discourage them from taking prescribed medication. Unfortunately, by following a layman's advice, the sufferers find that their conditions can return with all their previous intensity. On top of that, they feel guilty because they are convinced that "A.A. is against pills."

It becomes clear that just as it is wrong to enable or support any alcoholic to become readdicted to any drug, it's equally wrong to deprive any alcoholic of medication which can alleviate or control other disabling physical and/or emotional problems.

So it was O.K. for me to take the medication, and I did, for the next two years. It helped a lot with my depression. I was able to become familiar with the working of the 12 Steps and the program.

I am very grateful that I'm no longer plagued with depressions. My body chemistry has corrected itself, and I'm now able to enjoy what recovery has brought me.

WORTHLESS NO MORE
(MARIA LYNETTE C.—9 YEARS)

As far back as I can remember, I felt I was a completely worthless person. I had a lifetime of negative attitudes. I spent years in psychotherapy, which had little positive effect as I never once brought up the subject of my alcohol and drug use. I couldn't get much help from my therapist when I never told the whole truth.

It was only after a suicide attempt that I received the help I needed for my alcohol and drug addiction. I was clean and sober for a year before I began the real work on my depressions.

I found a psychiatrist who was familiar with the 12 Steps. By being honest, I began to see that from early childhood I felt I was bad and different from other people. I was full of guilt and shame, which produced self-hatred, resentments, and fear.

I stayed in therapy for a year and a half. Since then, studying the program, attending meetings, and my sponsor's guidance have helped me with my recovery from my addictions and depressions.

By working my program day by day, I receive the help from my Higher Power to keep negative thoughts in their proper perspective.

A THINKING PROBLEM
(CAROL S.—3 YEARS)

I came to the program because of my drinking problem, and stayed to learn I also had a thinking problem. I still get spells of depression, and it's the same negative feelings that I used to have. But what's different now is I can get free of the depression as soon as I want to. *Yes*, as soon as I want to. I'm lucky; I don't have any biological or genetic cause for my depressions.

There are three questions I ask myself when I get depressed. The first is, "Have I been eating the right foods for me, getting enough rest, and exercising?" Many times what I think is depression is really just not taking care of myself physically.

The second question is, "Have I been reaching out and helping other people without thinking about personal gain?"

The third question is, "Have I been thinking only of myself?"

When I look at these three questions, I usually find out what's causing my depression. It's because I've been thinking about myself again, or not taking care of myself physically, never because I'm thinking about someone else's problem.

THINGS I CAN'T CONTROL
(TONY B.–7 YEARS)

It took a while to be free of the depressions I brought with me to the program. I had the help of a very knowledgeable therapist, who helped me make some sense of my need to be in control of the people, places, and things in my life. I was fortunate my therapist was familiar with the 12 Step program. She applied the serenity prayer for me in ways I hadn't thought of.

I was able to describe the symptoms of my depression, but was confused as to which I could control and which were beyond my control. I spent years dwelling on my depression, trying to control things outside myself, and not taking any action to help myself. I kept digging myself into a hole, and when I reached bottom, I just kept digging.

In recovery, I learned that the things I *am* able to control are my attitudes, behaviors, diet, exercise, and how I act and react to other people's behavior.

I read somewhere that life showers challenging opportunities upon all of us. Some things we have no control over, so we accept them, learn and grow from them, and still do our best in spite of the odds. We commit ourselves to controlling those things we can, particularly ourselves. And if we do our best to be honest and humble, our Higher Power gives us the wisdom to know the difference.

BEING GOOD TO MYSELF
(KELLY H.—3-1/2 YEARS)

I've stopped punishing myself for not being perfect. I no longer expect perfection in everything I do, everything I think, and everything I say. All the time I spent blaming myself for not being perfect kept me wallowing in my depressions.

I needed time away from my addiction to get a clearer perspective on why I wasn't being good to myself. I realized I wasn't even being *fair* to myself. Anger and resentment kept me from my own needs. Of course, my sponsor, my friends in the fellowship, and working my program have helped me, but until I began taking care of myself I couldn't see the benefits.

GUILTY
(ROY C.–40 YEARS)

My sponsee picked me up a few weeks ago to go to a meeting. On the way, I told him what a bad day I'd had, and that I was really feeling depressed. I've been his sponsor for ten years, so he wasn't that taken aback by my admission. He understood that even after 40 years in A.A., I could still have a bad day and a temporary lapse in working my program.

I really don't remember what set it off, but I started thinking about the "I should haves and could haves," dwelling on mistakes I'd made, many during recovery. But there are benefits from being around the program so long—I wrote down what I was thinking and feeling guilty about.

When I had my list completed, I looked at it realistically and applied the Eighth and Ninth Steps to it. Did I need to make amends, forgive myself or others, or accept what I couldn't feasibly do anything about?

Writing it all down gave me a starting place for positive action, and a ladder to climb out of my depression.

TO GET OUT, YOU NEED TO WANT OUT
(PHILLIP F.–14 YEARS)

Over the years, I have been able to help many fellow members with their depressions. I'm no magician—I can't just say a few words and stop their depressions. But what I've been able to do is to help them give up their *need* to be depressed.

That may sound strange, but I have repeatedly run across people who don't want to be depressed, but at the same time have a reluctance to get away from depression.

The reluctance to work at not being depressed is the same as the reluctance I have seen among some members to work the Sixth and Seventh Steps. They feel there is something comfortable, familiar, and worthwhile in their depression and character defects.

When they understand they will have to ask their Higher Power and others for help, they begin to see recovery and reality as living in balance from extremes. To work through

depression and character defects, we first need
to want out, to want change, and to be ready to
do some work.

IF I LOVE YOU, HOW COME YOU DON'T LOVE ME?
(BETTY W.–2 YEARS)

Recovery has given me a new perspective. I am working toward a healthy
balance in my life. I'm grateful for all the new
information I've been given. There were so
many things I couldn't figure out on my own.

The angriest, most resentful time in my
life came when I was only three months in
recovery. I began to get a picture of how I had
put my value as a person into focusing too
much on others and ignoring my own feelings
and needs. My life had been one of constant
self-defeating behaviors that threw me into
deep depressions.

Until I became abstinent, I never took
care of my own needs or understood what was
in my best interest. I didn't feel good about
myself unless I was feeling good about what I
was doing for someone else. When I didn't get
back what I expected, I felt guilty. I would
start to ask myself, "*What's wrong with me?*"

The more I work at my relationship with myself, the more I make progress. Recovery has given me a way to face reality and not get stuck in the pain that sometimes comes when working the program.

TRYING TO FIGURE IT ALL OUT (JAMES L.—5 YEARS)

My first year clean and sober, I spent almost every waking minute trying to comprehend what was wrong with me. I thought if I knew the exact reasons I was depressed and miserable, then everything would be all right.

Instead of asking myself what I could do today for myself or others, I sat and brooded over all my problems. That led only to more fear, anxiety, and self-reproach.

When I was using, I was familiar with the literature on pills. In recovery, I read the psychiatric clinical literature, such as *Diagnostic and Statistical Manual of Mental Disorders*. I wanted the facts. What I got was more confused.

One week I thought I was Bipolar. The next I was Cyclothymic, then Dysthymic, then Atypical. Which check list of symptoms should I try this week? Then some weeks I was worried about my uptake of serotonin, or dopamine, or my endocrine system. Maybe I was hypoglycemic, hyperthyroid, or not taking enough vitamins?

What I finally learned from all my study was that I was the patient, not the doctor.

I am grateful to all the people in and out of the fellowship who have helped me with my depression. When I stopped trying to figure it all out, and accepted myself as someone prone to depression, I could move on and begin working through the down times.

STEP 12
(STEVE M.—1 YEAR)

Thank God, many in the program know that carrying the message also applies to those in the program who are still suffering. I certainly was suffering with depression until a few months ago.

I was helped by members who had, like myself, suffered from depression and were willing to say, "I've been there. Want to talk about it?" The advice to apply inventory-taking to my blue moods is still helping me. I'm getting some exercise, laying off the sugar, going to meetings where I participate, and involving myself in activities with other people.

CHEER UP!
(JENNIFER T.—7 YEARS)

It never helped me, when I was depressed, to have fellow members tell me to cheer up and snap out of it. It was worse when a member told me I "must not be working the program properly." All of them meant well, but they didn't fully understand because they had little personal knowledge of depression.

Those of us in recovery are lucky, however, because many people in and out of the program *do* understand about depression. I was helped when a friend told me to apply the 12 Steps to my depressions the way I had applied them to my addiction. The same friend also told me it was O.K. to seek professional counseling.

These two things have helped me the most in reducing my depressions: remembering to stop punishing myself with my own mind, and to constantly keep my expectations in perspective.

The program teaches us that we "are not saints," that we work for "progress, not perfection," and that "although we may not be a famous somebody, we aren't nobodies."

THIRD STEP
(CHRIS E.—6 YEARS)

During the last four years in the program, I have not had a major depression. I've had bad days, angry times, periods of growth and change, but I know the difference now between those and depression.

Before the program, I was always depressed. I thought I would have to live my life that way. I loved the effect alcohol and drugs gave me; when I didn't feel good, I just got drunk or wasted. I went to doctors to get pills for my nerves (or so I said). I spent years on the merry-go-round of feeling depressed, feeling worthless, and self-medicating.

I finally made it into the program. I spent the first two years clean and sober, but still suffered from depression. Around that time, I heard a woman tell her story at a meeting and made the effort to talk to her afterwards.

She'd spent her first eighteen months in recovery going to meetings, working the program, and still feeling depressed. She pointed out to me that I was staying abstinent because I had comprehended and been working the program just on the First and Second Steps. I had heard and thought I knew all about the

Third Step, but with her help I realized I really didn't understand it or use it at all.

I knew I was powerless over my addiction, that the program was a greater power in my life, and that I was being restored to sanity, but I was frozen on really taking the Third Step. I was waiting for it to just happen to me, not knowing I had to take the action first.

The Third Step isn't a magic pill you just take and you're there. First you need to be willing, and then you need to get busy. I now understand why it was so difficult for me. I needed to change, to live my life differently, and to follow directions.

WORKING THROUGH
(BELINDA R.–6 YEARS)

I took a while to adjust from the physical withdrawal of my addiction. When I began to feel better physically, my emotions and thinking caught up with what was happening. Wow! Was I depressed! All I could do was think about my past and feel anger, resentment, and fear. Was that what recovery was, going from the *fast* lane to the *past* lane? The pain was too much. And what about this gigantic chip on my shoulder?

I was very close to relapse, or to actually putting into action my thoughts of suicide. There was no single magical event that brought me out of and through this terrible time in early recovery. I learned in treatment how important it was to ask for help, but I took my time before I did it!

I owe a great deal to my sponsor. She got me to start working through my pain and to begin to see the healing available in working the 12 Steps. My life had been one of being split off from myself. Most of my character defects were learned as a child in order to cope and survive.

I could probably write a book on what happened to me before recovery and after, but I'll just give you some of the highlights of what I've learned.

Maybe I never really had much of a chance to lead a "normal" life. Things were done to me that shouldn't happen to anyone, ever. The Steps have led me out of focusing on those awful negative events to focusing on what I can do, with the help of my friends and my Higher Power.

I've been able to forgive others and myself, to acknowledge and accept what I can do today. When I based my outlook and moods on the bad things in the past, I went nowhere. I denied myself the possibility of a better today, a better tomorrow.

I won't tell you that just thinking positive thoughts is the way to get away from self-pity, self-blame, and self-hatred, but it is part of it. First, I had to want out, then I had to get help, and finally, I had to get to work, with the awareness I had to *act* my way out instead of *thinking* my way out. I had to go through the pain, not around it.

I *can* tell you that a whole load of pain has gone away by itself, by my staying with the program, staying willing to do the work, and exerting the effort to help myself.

4

PRACTICAL WAYS THAT HELP

CHANGE THE THINGS I CAN

When we're depressed, it is difficult to motivate ourselves into action and activities that will help us out of our depression. Thinking there is nothing we can do only adds to our negative feelings.

Even those who are taking antidepressant medication need to take practical steps to work out of depression. The following is a summary of the actions taken by our group of interviewees which have assisted them with their down times.

ASKING FOR HELP

If we believe we can be helped out of our depression and want to be helped, we need to ask for help. Depression has to be brought out into the open and talked about. We can ask our friends, sponsor, counselor, therapist, or a relative for help.

Professional help from an individual familiar with 12 Step recovery is important. We need to remain open to the possibility we may have an imbalance in body chemistry that calls for nonaddictive, nonmood-altering, antidepressant medication. We can talk to older members who have gone through what we're experiencing, as well as newer ones who remind us of how far we've come.

Acknowledging and accepting our feelings is important. Trying to understand where these feelings come from and what causes them helps us deal with old history that may be contributing to depression.

LOWERING EXPECTATIONS

When there is too wide a gap between standards we set for ourselves and our actual achievements, we add to our unhappiness. The 12 Steps teach us to be true to ourselves and become aware of what we are capable of doing.

There is no quicker way to undermine our progress than to place unrealistic demands on ourselves.

When we lower our expectations, we also deemphasize our faults and build self-esteem.

ACTION IS NECESSARY

There is a slogan in the program that says, "Willingness without action is fantasy." When we motivate ourselves (which isn't easy when we're depressed), and are willing to work on our depression, we need to take the appropriate action.

Again and again, we are told that our recovery program is, above all, one of action. We are reminded that "nobody can do it for you, but you can't do it alone." The same premise applies to working through our depressions. We need other people to help us.

PROFESSIONAL HELP

Many of us have been helped by professionals, psychiatrists, psychologists, counselors, and the clergy. Many of us are enjoying our recovery because of that help. Professional help may be what we need for the best possible recovery. Three guidelines have proved important:

1. Find a professional who is familiar with addictions and 12 Step recovery.
2. Work the program even when seeing or being helped by a professional.
3. Be honest and open with the counselor or therapist.

OVERDEPENDENCE

When we base our happiness on external objects, we are working at staying stuck in depression. We can't fix our shortcomings by buying things, taking geographical cures, or trying to manipulate or control others.

If it were within our capacity to fix other people's lives, we would have done so a long time ago with all our friends and relatives. We finally realized in our First Step how hopelessly outmatched we were for the job of fixing ourselves and the whole world. Most of us struggled for years to fix our own lives, but we couldn't. It wasn't until we admitted we were licked that we finally got the help we needed. What is true for staying abstinent is also true for our depressions. When we work the other Eleven Steps, we realize with the help of our Higher Power and others we can work for solutions.

The program teaches us what we need to depend on. We are encouraged to accept situations (people, places, and things) we cannot change. We are told to work on the situations we can change.

When we are overdependent on externals and try to fix people and things, it doesn't work very well. All we really can do is focus on fixing ourselves.

OPEN MINDS

"Minds are like parachutes: they won't work unless they're open." "When your head begins to swell, your mind stops growing." These two 12 Step slogans point out another cause of depression.

Unless we maintain open minds, we cannot hope to make attitude changes for the better. Open-mindedness helps prevent self-centeredness and reduces the possibility of hanging on to painful resentments. Open minds do not allow intolerance or prejudice.

When we lock the doors of our mind, we close our hearts as well. Many of us, in the days before we began recovery, believed we knew everything. We kept our minds closed to new information. We knew what we knew and that was enough.

In recovery, we know we **don't** know everything. What a relief! With an open mind, we stop focusing on ourselves (the problem) and work on learning (the solution).

The program slogan "H.O.W. = Honesty, Open-mindedness, Willingness" is a pattern for character and spiritual growth. It is also an aid for working through depression.

H.A.L.T.

In our Fellowship, we have seen many men and women recover from low and terrible bottoms. The signposts to relapse and depression are clearly marked.

Don't get too **H**ungry. When we're physically weak, it affects our attitudes and spiritual life. When hungry, eat.

Don't get too **A**ngry. We need to stay away from anger altogether. Anger is the breeder of resentments. We have been eaten alive by our grudges. Cool off.

Don't get too **L**onely. Loneliness makes us an easy mark for the voices that tempt us away from our Program. When we feel loneliness coming on, we need to go to a meeting or use the phone.

Don't get too **T**ired. When we're tired, it's easy for us to remember the chemical pick-me-ups we relied on. When we're tired, we need to rest.

Eating the right foods, staying calm, using the Fellowship, and resting are tools for avoiding depression.

GROWING UP

Most people in recovery can say they had very long childhoods. We often hear, "The first 30 years of my childhood nearly killed me." Carrying over to our adult lives childish egos and immature attitudes can keep us depressed.

We add to self-pity when we refuse to give up our child-like needs of control and our desire that all our needs be met. Motives of power, attention, and instant pleasure have no place in our program. They can keep us frustrated and depressed.

Working on depression teaches us ways to deal with our scared little child. At the same time, we learn to nurture the child within us. When we act like babies, we believe we are the center of the world. We think status, fame, money, and beauty will make us happy because they are the most important things in the world.

Dealing with our depressions helps put our childish attitudes behind us. We change from believing totally in ourselves and Baby Power to believing in our Higher Power. We take responsibility for our attitudes and get busy working on self-discovery, self-acceptance, self-discipline, and self-forgiveness.

HELPING OTHERS

Helping and serving others takes us away from thinking of ourselves. One of the first things we learn in recovery is that we are people who need people.

We lighten our depressions when we reach out and ask for help, and also when we share with others. We overcome our "terminal uniqueness," isolation, and feelings of "being alone in a crowd."

One of the paradoxes of recovery is that to keep what we have been given and to enjoy the benefits of recovery, we have to "give it away." When we learn to give and to help others without seeking credit, we find the reality of our Fellowship: by giving, we are also keeping.

Many members have reported that reaching out to someone who is suffering or confused and saying, "Is there anything I can do to help?" takes them out of their depression.

PHYSICAL

During down times and depression, we need to be concerned with our physical well-being. Depression is usually characterized by having little or no energy. If we neglect ourselves by not keeping ourselves and our living area clean, eating the wrong foods, or not exercising, we add to our depression. When we take care of our health, get regular medical checkups, and take vitamins, we add to our chances of avoiding depression.

Be good to yourself. Do little things to please yourself, just as you would to please someone else you love. Pamper yourself with dinner out, a long soothing bubble bath, an evening alone with a good book. Structure your time to include things and actions that give you pleasure. Laugh. Relax.

POSITIVE THINKING

The thoughts we have, the way we talk to ourselves, and what we believe about ourselves are major factors in producing, avoiding, or getting out of depression.

This doesn't mean that the answer lies totally in positive thinking, but certainly it is *part* of the answer.

Taking a daily inventory of our negative thoughts and writing them down can clearly point out self-defeating attitudes. As we get an idea how our stinking thinking adds to our down time, we must get into action. We need to "act as if" and begin talking to ourselves in a positive way, even (or especially) when it is difficult to do so.

The program says, "utilize, don't analyze." If our inventory-taking shows us we could use improvement with our self-talk, that information needs to be acted upon, not analyzed.

We have to exert some effort to correct our thinking and not stay stuck dwelling on our negative points.

Spiritual

In our 12 Step program, we come to believe in a Power greater than ourselves. Each member has their own conception of this Higher Power. The majority feel comfortable calling this Power God. We began our spiritual journey in recovery by discovering a Power *other* than ourselves because we weren't God.

We can be helped with our depressions through our belief in a Higher Power and through prayer. Some of the prayers and meditations that have helped us are reprinted here in Chapter 6.

5

EMOTIONAL SOBRIETY/
RECOVERY

THE NEXT FRONTIER:
EMOTIONAL SOBRIETY
BILL W.

I think that many oldsters who have put our AA "booze cure" to severe but successful tests still find they often lack emotional sobriety. Perhaps they will be the spearhead for the next major development in AA—the development of much more real maturity and balance (which is to say, humility) in our relations with ourselves, with our fellows, and with God.

Those adolescent urges that so many of us have for top approval, perfect security, and perfect romance—urges quite appropriate to age seventeen—prove to be an impossible way of life when we are at age forty-seven or fifty-seven.

Since AA began, I've taken immense wallops in all these areas because of my failure to grow up, emotionally and spiritually. My

God, how painful it is to keep demanding the impossible, and how very painful to discover, finally, that all along we have had the cart before the horse! Then comes the final agony of seeing how awfully wrong we have been, but still finding ourselves unable to get off the emotional merry-go-round.

How to translate a right mental conviction into a right emotional result, and so into easy, happy, and good living—well, that's not only the neurotic's problem, it's the problem of life itself for all of us who have got to the point of real willingness to hew to right principles in all our affairs.

Even then, as we hew away, peace and joy may still elude us. That's the place so many of us AA oldsters have come to. And it's a hell of a spot, literally. How shall our unconscious—from which so many of our fears, compulsions, and phony aspirations still stream—be brought into line with what we actually believe, know, and want! How to convince our dumb, raging, and hidden "Mr. Hyde" becomes our main task.

I've recently come to believe that this can be achieved. I believe so because I begin to see many benighted ones—folks like you and me—commencing to get results. Last autumn, depression, having no really rational cause at all, almost took me to the cleaners. I began to be scared that I was in for another long chronic spell. Considering the grief I've had with depressions, it wasn't a bright prospect.

I kept asking myself, "Why can't the Twelve Steps work to release depression?" By the hour, I stared at the St. Francis Prayer . . . "It's better to comfort than to be comforted." Here was the formula, all right. But why didn't it work?

Suddenly I realized what the matter was. My basic flaw had always been dependence—almost absolute dependence—on people or circumstances to supply me with prestige, security, and the like. Failing to get these things according to my perfectionist dreams and specifications, I had fought for them. And when defeat came, so did my depression.

There wasn't a chance of making the outgoing love of St. Francis a workable and joyous way of life until these fatal and almost absolute dependencies were cut away.

Because I had over the years undergone a little spiritual development, the *absolute* quality of these frightful dependencies had never before been so starkly revealed. Reinforced by what grace I could secure in prayer, I found I had to exert every ounce of will and action to cut off these faulty emotional dependencies upon people, upon AA, indeed, upon any set of circumstances whatsoever. Then only could I be free to love as Francis had. Emotional and instinctual satisfactions, I saw, were really the extra dividends of having love, offering love, and expressing a love appropriate to each relation of life.

Plainly, I could not avail myself of God's love until I was able to offer it back to Him by loving others as He would have me. And I couldn't possibly do that so long as I was victimized by false dependencies.

For my dependency meant demand—a demand for the possession and control of the people and conditions surrounding me.

While those words "absolute dependency" may look like a gimmick, they were the ones that helped to trigger my release into my present degree of stability and quietness of mind, qualities which I am now trying to consolidate by offering love to others regardless of the return to me.

This seems to be the primary healing circuit: an outgoing love of God's creation and His people, by means of which we avail ourselves of His love for us. It is most clear that the real current can't flow until our paralyzing dependencies are broken, and broken at depth.

Only then can we possibly have a glimmer of what adult love really is.

Spiritual calculus, you say? Not a bit of it. Watch any AA of six months working with a new Twelfth Step case. If the case says "To the devil with you," the twelfth-stepper only smiles and turns to another case. He doesn't feel frustrated or rejected. If his next case responds, and in turn starts to give love and attention to other alcoholics yet gives none back to him, the sponsor is happy about it anyway. He still doesn't feel rejected; instead he rejoices that his one-time prospect is sober and happy. And if his next following case turns out in later time to be his best friend (or romance), then the sponsor is most joyful. But he well knows that his happiness is a byproduct—the extra dividend of giving without any demand for a return.

The really stabilizing thing for him was having and offering love to that strange drunk on his doorstep. That was Francis at work, powerful and practical, minus dependency and minus demand.

In the first six months of my own sobriety, I worked hard with many alcoholics. Not a one responded. Yet this work kept me sober. It wasn't a question of those alcoholics giving me anything. My stability came out of trying to give, not out of demanding that I receive.

Thus I think it can work out with emotional sobriety. If we examine every disturbance we have, great or small, we will find at the root of it some unhealthy dependency and its consequent unhealthy demand. Let us, with God's help, continually surrender these hobbling demands. Then we can be set free to live and love; we may then be able to Twelfth Step ourselves and others into emotional sobriety.

Of course I haven't offered you a really new idea—only a gimmick that has started to unhook several of my own "hexes" at depth. Nowadays, my brain no longer races compulsively in either elation, grandiosity, or depression. I have been given a quiet place in bright sunshine.

A.A. *Grapevine*, January 1958
(Copyright © by The A.A. Grapevine, Inc.
Reprinted with permission.)

IN SEARCH OF
EMOTIONAL SOBRIETY
ANONYMOUS

About a year ago I read an article written by Bill W. titled "The Next Frontier:

Emotional Sobriety." He wrote this article late in his AA recovery and it deals with that wonderfully terrifying realm—beyond not drinking. To me, it was the most powerful thing he ever wrote, along with the Big Book. It opened up a whole new dimension of recovery I was struggling to find. It literally saved my life.

After almost three and one-half years in AA, living without my medication—alcohol—I came to a crisis in my recovery. I ended up going back to alcohol for a short period because of the pain and despair I was feeling. It was worse than anything I had experienced up to that time because I had nowhere to hide from it. My emotions were stalking me into the deepest depression of my life.

I see now that I drank all those previous years to stay sane. Year by year I had become more uncomfortable emotionally even though I continued to go to four or five meetings a week, read, pray, meditate, and really work Steps One, Ten, Eleven, and Twelve. I talked constantly with my AA friends and others about how I felt. I was in a state of despair and self-condemnation for failing to "work the program." The harder I tried, the worse I felt. I could not find serenity or emotional balance. I could not figure out what was wrong and no one seemed to know what to tell me except to go to meetings, read the Big Book, and get off the pity pot.

It was then that I discovered the article by Bill W. My eyes and heart and soul were opened up to that "new frontier" he had discovered after his long, agonizing, dry search through depression. I realized at once that he had suffered the same emotional devastation that I had—what he called an "emotional merry-go-round." He stated the problem this way: "How to translate a right mental conviction into a right emotional result, and so into easy, happy, and good living . . . . It's the problem of life itself for all of us who have got to the point of real willingness to hew to right principles in all our affairs."

There is a "point," as he calls it, where I am willing, but for some reason unable, to get past a block that prevents me from choosing to be happy and journey on into emotional sobriety. Bill W. aptly called it "a hell of a spot!" He also showed me I was dealing with my unconscious, that great expanse of old recordings which continually plays a lifetime of neglect, frustration, and fear. Locked in this deep hidden part of me are fears and compulsions which he calls "faulty and emotional dependencies upon people, upon AA, indeed, upon any set of circumstances whatever." This was a powerful and revealing statement about my dilemma, my recovery, and the direction I should now go. I was still absolutely dependent for validation and security on people (even my long-dead parents) and circumstances beyond my control. This created a terrible endless spiral of self-condemnation, guilt, and depression.

I began to see that my recovery was a process of growth followed by sabotage. These episodes began with a kind of innocence and newness of experience offered to me by my recovery—a pink cloud, if you will. From this new experience, I was allowed to make positive choices and responses, thus creating joy and excitement in my life. As this high peaked out, I felt the need for relief and rest. To find this relief I chose the opposite of the positive and joyous feelings. This was how I nurtured myself; it was all I had ever learned.

Of course, this caused decline instead of peace and so my need for relief grew. I added other opposites and experienced more decline. Frustration and doubt began to set in. Soon I slipped into a kind of learned violence against myself for failing in my attempts to grow and nurture myself. From here it was only a short slide to depression, that gray expanse of self-hatred and self-deceit. After periods of depression, the episodes would start over again with some new experience. My absolute dependencies on people and circumstances were sabotaging my recovery with a type of self-abuse.

Bill W. goes on to say that the answer is love, "an outgoing love of God's creation and His people, by means of which we avail ourselves of His love for us." He says that something very powerful must now take place if I am ever to achieve the emotional sobriety this kind of love can bring: "It is most clear that the real current can't flow until our paralyzing dependencies are broken and broken at depth."

This is now the new frontier of recovery I am beginning. It is a frightening, painful, and glorious journey into freedom—a plunge into depths of emotions and feelings I had never achieved. But out of all the pain and grieving of breaking those dependencies comes a love of self and others that is beyond imagining. It is a deep and powerful Ninth Step of amends to myself and those I had so depended on.

As I begin this journey of "breaking at depth," through reading, treatment, therapy, meetings, and the Twelve Steps, I am finding a healing beyond description. It is a bonding and reuniting with myself, with others, and with that inner light I call my Higher Power. Once again Bill W.'s words come to mind to guide me and help me go to any length to recover: "More and more we regard all who labor in the total field of alcoholism as our companions on a march from darkness into light. We see that we can accomplish together what we could never accomplish in separation and in rivalry."

It is the wonderful searching and open-mindedness of this that has helped prevent me from suffering and the destructive recovery-robbing consequences of "contempt prior to investigation."

I believe many of us AAs are entering the new frontier called emotional sobriety that Bill W. was beginning to sense and discover for himself years ago. Abstinence from alcohol is truly only the beginning of an incredible spiritual journey into healing and joy. And I thank my Higher Power that I have Bill W. and others to travel with me.

A.A. *Grapevine*, May 1989
(Copyright © by The A.A. Grapevine, Inc. Reprinted with permission.)

6

PRAYERS AND MEDITATIONS

SERENITY PRAYER

GOD, grant me the SERENITY to accept the things I cannot change; the COURAGE to change the things I can; and the WISDOM to know the difference.

THE BLUES

How do you know when you've hit bottom? When you stop digging! —Anonymous

We learn in recovery how to deal with the down times. Our program constantly reminds us that we hit bottom when we stop digging. Therefore we can stop a downward spiral by simply letting go and letting God catch us in the palm of His hand. Our Higher Power and the program will provide a ladder with which we can crawl out of our hole. We just need to remember to use the ladder.

God will never take away our free will. If we use our will to do the business of our

Higher Power and work the Steps, we will be surrounded by love and have strength. It is when we sometimes use our free will to do the bidding of our own ego and set expectations too high that we fall into a bottomless pit.

Working with and helping others is the basic "ladder" at my disposal when I deal with the blues and down times. So I always keep in touch with my fellow travelers.

Prayer Of Saint Francis Assisi

Lord, make me an instrument of Your peace!
Where there is hatred, let me sow love.
Where there is injury, pardon.
Where there is doubt, faith.
Where there is despair, hope.
Where there is darkness, light.
Where there is sadness, joy.
O Divine Master, grant that I
may not so much seek
To be consoled as to console.
To be understood as to understand.
To be loved as to love.
For it is in giving that we receive.
It is in pardoning that we are pardoned.
It is in dying that we are born to eternal life.

DEPRESSIONS

Don't look down unless you plan on staying there. —Anonymous

Depressions and setbacks are a part of life for us even when we are solidly active in the program. We were told early that an addict's highs are always higher than the ordinary and their lows lower. When things begin going wrong (and the law of averages predicts that things will), we can feel depressed even when we compare these lows with the good feelings we experience when we grow spiritually.

At times of depression, we can find relief and change our attitude by entering into the caring and sharing of our program. It is certain that we can never overcome our down times alone and without help. We always remind ourselves that depressions will not fade unless we have the help of others, sometimes professional help. Many are also helped with the blues when they get out of themselves and help others.

To handle my depressions and low points, I need the help of my friends in the program. I can't do it alone.

TODAY'S THOUGHT

I am but one, but I am one;
I can't do everything,
But I can do SOMETHING;
What I can do, I ought to do,
What I ought to do, God helping me,
I WILL DO.

ASKING FOR HELP

The smartest thing a 12 Step member can say is, "Help me." —Anonymous

The weight of carrying the world on our backs has been removed from us in recovery. It is good to remember the world was never ours to carry in the first place. Our program prevents us from setting ourselves up for failure. Most of us are used to being the Lone Ranger. Instead of silver bullets, we left empty lives. Our solitude taught us never to ask for help, always to go it alone. Our isolation produced a pitiful figure we would dress up in toughness.

This, of course, was phony, because inside we were anything but tough. When we operate alone, pretending to be strong and in control, we set ourselves in motion to experience depression and pain. Stinking thinking flourishes in isolation. The key to unlocking the many gifts of the fellowship is asking for help. There is strength, wisdom, hope, all waiting for us if we ask for help.

I have learned to ask for help and to help when I am asked.

TO BE HONEST

Higher Power, help me to be honest with myself. It is so easy to alibi, to make excuses for my shortcomings. It is so easy to blame others and circumstances as a child does. Help me to see myself honestly: a human being who needs You this day and every day. Help me to surrender my weak will to Your strength.

LIMITATIONS

The four "A"s: Acceptance, Awareness, Action, Attitude. —Anonymous

It is as important for us to live within our limitations as it is to live up to our capabilities. Step One tells us that we do not have a limit but that we are limited. We admit this when we begin our growth in our Twelve Steps. The action Step, the final one, reminds us that we practice the principles of our program in all our affairs.

And, of course, we accept the truth that we seek spiritual progress, not spiritual perfection. In admitting limitations we are reminding ourselves that we are only human. When we keep ourselves from trying to play God, we admit our imperfections. We seek our Higher Power's help in lessening our limitations when we take inventories and remember the four "A"s: Acceptance, Awareness, Action, and Attitude.

My program is based on my learning to live with my limitations. I will also remember that I need to live up to my capabilities.

PRAYER FOR PROTECTION

The light of God surrounds me;
The love of God enfolds me;
The power of God protects me;
The presence of God watches over me;
Wherever I am, God is!

ALTERNATIVES

A person is usually not attached to anything more than their own suffering. —Anonymous

We all have a choice between widely separated alternatives. We can like ourselves or hate ourselves. We can lift ourselves up or put ourselves down. We can be for ourselves